I Know an Old Lady

by ROSE BONNE

Music by ALAN MILLS

Pictures by ABNER GRABOFF

SCHOLASTIC INC.
New York Toronto London Auckland Sydney

ISBN 0-590-02967-3

7/9

Printed in the U.S.A.

23

I know an old lady who swallowed a fly.
I don't know why she swallowed a fly!
I guess she'll die!

I know an old lady who swallowed a spider
That wriggled and wriggled and tickled inside
  her.
She swallowed the spider to catch the fly,
But I don't know why she swallowed the fly!
I guess she'll die!

I know an old lady who swallowed a bird.
Now how absurd, to swallow a bird!
She swallowed the bird to catch the spider
That wriggled and wriggled and tickled inside
    her.
She swallowed the spider to catch the fly,
But I don't know why she swallowed the fly!
I guess she'll die!

I know an old lady who swallowed a cat.
Now fancy that, to swallow a cat!

She swallowed the cat to catch the bird.

She swallowed the bird to catch the spider

That wriggled and wriggled and tickled inside
   her.

She swallowed the spider to catch the fly,

But I don't know why she swallowed the fly!

I guess she'll die!

MEN
WORK
ING

I know an old lady who swallowed a dog.
My, what a hog to swallow a dog!

She swallowed the dog to catch the cat.

She swallowed the cat to catch the bird.
She swallowed the bird to catch the spider
That wriggled and wriggled and tickled inside
  her.
She swallowed the spider to catch the fly,
But I don't know why she swallowed the fly!

I guess she'll die!

I know an old lady who swallowed a goat.

Just opened her throat, and in walked the goat!

She
swallowed
the goat
to
catch
the
dog.

She
swallowed
the dog
to
catch
the cat.

She
swallowed
the cat
to
catch
the bird.

She
swallowed
the bird
to
catch
the spider

That wriggled and wriggled
and tickled inside her.
She swallowed the spider
to catch the fly,
But I don't know why
she swallowed the fly!
I guess she'll die!

I know an old lady who swallowed a cow.
I don't know how she swallowed a cow!

She
swallowed
the cow
to
catch
the goat.

She
swallowed
the goat
to
catch the dog.

She
swallowed
the dog
to
catch the cat.

She swallowed the cat to catch the bird.

She swallowed the bird to catch the spider

That wriggled and wriggled and tickled inside
  her.

She swallowed the spider to catch the fly,

But I don't know why she swallowed the fly!

I guess she'll die!

I know
an old lady
who swallowed a

Horse!

She's dead,

of
Course!

I Know an Old Lady

Words by
ROSE BONNE

Music by
ALAN MILLS

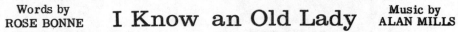

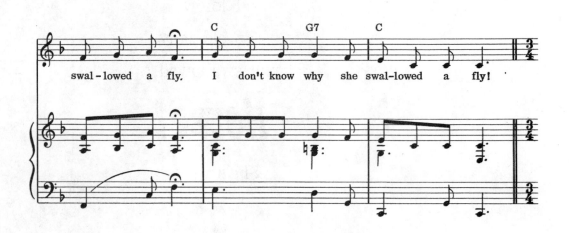

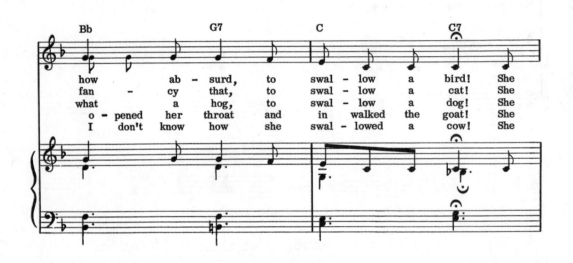